People in My Community/La gente de mi comunidad

Librarian/
El bibliotecario

Jacqueline Laks Gorman
photographs by/fotografías de Gregg Andersen

Reading consultant/Consultora de lectura: Susan Nations, M.Ed., author/literacy coach/consultant

Please visit our web site at: www.garethstevens.com
For a free color catalog describing Weekly Reader® Early Learning Library's
list of high-quality books, call 1-877-445-5824 (USA) or 1-800-387-3178 (Canada).
Weekly Reader® Early Learning Library's fax: (414) 336-0164.

Library of Congress Cataloging-in-Publication Data

Gorman, Jacqueline Laks, 1955-
   [Librarian. Spanish & English]
   Librarian = El bibliotecario / by Jacqueline Laks Gorman.
     p. cm. — (People in my community = La gente de mi comunidad)
   Summary: Photographs and simple text in English and Spanish describe
the work done by librarians.
   Includes bibliographical references and index.
   ISBN 0-8368-3310-4 (lib. bdg.)
   ISBN 0-8368-3344-9 (softcover)
   1. Librarians—Juvenile literature. 2. Libraries—Juvenile literature.
[1. Librarians. 2. Occupations. 3. Spanish language materials—Bilingual.]
I. Title: Bibliotecario. II. Title.
Z682.G6818   2002
020—dc21   2002066351

Updated and reprinted in 2006.
This edition first published in 2002 by
Weekly Reader® Early Learning Library
A member of the WRC Media Family of Companies
330 West Olive Street, Suite 100
Milwaukee, WI 53212 USA

Art direction and page layout: Tammy West
Photographer: Gregg Andersen
Editorial assistant: Diane Laska-Swanke
Production: Susan Ashley
Translators: Tatiana Acosta and Guillermo Gutiérrez

Printed in the United States of America

7 8 9 10 09 08 07 06

Note to Educators and Parents

Reading is such an exciting adventure for young children! They are beginning to integrate their oral language skills with written language. To encourage children along the path to early literacy, books must be colorful, engaging, and interesting; they should invite the young reader to explore both the print and the pictures.

People in My Community is a new series designed to help children read about the world around them. In each book young readers will learn interesting facts about some familiar community helpers.

Each book is specially designed to support the young reader in the reading process. The familiar topics are appealing to young children and invite them to read — and re-read — again and again. The full-color photographs and enhanced text further support the student during the reading process.

In addition to serving as wonderful picture books in schools, libraries, homes, and other places where children learn to love reading, these books are specifically intended to be read within an instructional guided reading group. This small group setting allows beginning readers to work with a fluent adult model as they make meaning from the text. After children develop fluency with the text and content, the book can be read independently. Children and adults alike will find these books supportive, engaging, and fun!

Una nota a los educadores y a los padres

¡La lectura es una emocionante aventura para los niños! En esta etapa están comenzando a integrar su manejo del lenguaje oral con el lenguaje escrito. Para fomentar la lectura desde una temprana edad, los libros deben ser vistosos, atractivos e interesantes; deben invitar al joven lector a explorar tanto el texto como las ilustraciones.

La gente de mi comunidad es una nueva serie pensada para ayudar a los niños a conocer el mundo que los rodea. En cada libro, los jóvenes lectores conocerán datos interesantes sobre el trabajo de distintas personas de la comunidad.

Cada libro ha sido especialmente diseñado para facilitar el proceso de lectura. La familiaridad con los temas tratados atrae la atención de los niños y los invita a leer — y releer — una y otra vez. Las fotografías a todo color y el tipo de letra facilitan aún más al estudiante el proceso de lectura.

Además de servir como fantásticos libros ilustrados en la escuela, la biblioteca, el hogar y otros lugares donde los niños aprenden a amar la lectura, estos libros han sido concebidos específicamente para ser leídos en grupos de instrucción guiada. Este contexto de grupos pequeños permite que los niños que se inician en la lectura trabajen con un adulto cuya fluidez les sirve de modelo para comprender el texto. Una vez que se han familiarizado con el texto y el contenido, los niños pueden leer los libros por su cuenta. ¡Tanto niños como adultos encontrarán que estos libros son útiles, entretenidos y divertidos!

— Susan Nations, M.Ed., author, literacy coach,
and consultant in literacy development

The librarian has an important job. The librarian helps people.

– – – – – – – –

El trabajo de la bibliotecaria es muy importante. La bibliotecaria ayuda a la gente.

The librarian works in the library. The librarian works with books.

– – – – – – – –

La bibliotecaria trabaja en la biblioteca. La bibliotecaria trabaja con libros.

PUBLIC LIBRARY AND READING

120

OPEN

The librarian knows a lot about books. She decides what books to buy for the library.

- - - - - - - -

La bibliotecaria sabe mucho de libros. Es quien decide qué libros comprar para la biblioteca.

The librarian puts the books on the **shelves**. Each book has to go in the right place.

– – – – – – – –

La bibliotecaria pone los libros en los **estantes**. Cada libro tiene su lugar.

shelves/estantes

11

When you visit the library, the librarian helps you. She answers all your questions.

Cuando vas a la biblioteca, la bibliotecaria te ayuda. Responde a todas tus preguntas.

Do you know what book you want? The librarian can help you find it.

— — — — — — —

¿Sabes qué libro quieres? La bibliotecaria te puede ayudar a encontrarlo.

Do you want to take a book home? The librarian can help you get a **library card**.

- - - - - - - -

¿Quieres llevarte un libro a casa? La bibliotecaria te puede ayudar a obtener una **tarjeta de la biblioteca**.

library card/tarjeta de la biblioteca

The librarian checks
out all your books and
tells you when to bring
them back.

- - - - - - - -

La bibliotecaria te
entrega los libros
que quieres sacar y
te dice cuándo debes
devolverlos.

19

It looks like fun to be a librarian. Would you like to be a librarian some day?

- - - - - - -

Ser bibliotecaria parece divertido. ¿Te gustaría ser bibliotecaria algún día?

Glossary/Glosario

librarian — a person who works in a library

bibliotecaria — persona que trabaja en una biblioteca

library — a place where people can use or borrow magazines, books, videos and other things

biblioteca — lugar donde la gente puede consultar o pedir prestados libros, videos, revistas y otras cosas

library card — a special card that is used by someone to check things out of a library

tarjeta de la biblioteca — una tarjeta especial que se usa para sacar cosas de la biblioteca

shelves — thin pieces of wood or metal that hold books

estantes — láminas de madera o metal sobre las que se ponen libros

For More Information/Más información

Fiction Books/Libros de ficción

Deedy, Carmen Agra. *The Library Dragon*. Atlanta: Peachtree, 1994.

Williams, Suzanne. *Library Lil*. New York: Dial, 1997.

Nonfiction Books/Libros de no ficción

Flanagan, Alice K. *Ms. Davison, Our Librarian*. New York: Children's Press, 1997.

Kottke, Jan. *A Day with a Librarian*. New York: Children's Press, 2000.

Web Sites/Páginas Web

What Does a Librarian Do?

www.whatdotheydo.com/libraria.htm

For information on a librarian's job

KidsConnect

www.ala.org/ICONN/AskKC.html

Send an email question to a real librarian, and get an answer back

Index/Índice

books, 6, 8, 10,
    14, 16, 18
libros

borrowing books,
    16, 18
sacar libros

checking out
    books, 18
sacar libros

library, 6, 8, 12
biblioteca

library card, 16, 17
tarjeta de la
    biblioteca

shelves, 10, 11
estantes

visiting the library, 12
visitar la biblioteca

work of the
    librarian, 4, 6,
    8, 10, 12, 14,
    16, 18
trabajo de la
    bibliotecaria

About the Author/Información sobre la autora

Jacqueline Laks Gorman is a writer and editor. She grew up in New York City and began her career working on encyclopedias and other reference books. Since then, she has worked on many different kinds of books. She lives with her husband and children, Colin and Caitlin, in DeKalb, Illinois.

Jacqueline Laks Gorman es escritora y editora. Creció en Nueva York, y se inició en su profesión editando enciclopedias y otros libros de consulta. Desde entonces ha trabajado en muchos tipos de libros. Vive con su esposo y sus hijos, Colin y Caitlin, en DeKalb, Illinois.